Who Was the Woman Who Wore the Hat?

written and illustrated by

NANCY PATZ

WITHDRAWN

DUTTON BOOKS

NEW YORK

page 13: This photo appears in the *Tower of Life* [exhibit] at the
United States Holocaust Memorial Museum in Washington, D.C.,
and belongs to the Yaffa Eliach Shtetl Collection.
page 19: Collection of the Netherlands Institute for War
Documentation, Amsterdam
pages 22, 23, 24, & 25: Collection of Yad Vashem, the Holocaust
Martyrs' and Heroes' Remembrance, Jerusalem
page 31: Collection Jewish Historical Museum, Amsterdam

CIP Data is available.
Published in the United States 2003 by Dutton Books,
a member of Penguin Putnam Inc.
345 Hudson Street, New York, New York 10014
www.penguinputnam.com
Designed by Alyssa Morris and Irene Vandervoort
Printed in China
First Edition
1 3 5 7 9 10 8 6 4 2
ISBN 0-525-46999-0

To the memory of

my mother

and my father

———

To Susan L. Roth — my thanks beyond words

And my warmest appreciation to: the experts at Dutton —
president and publisher (and my editor and friend)
Stephanie Owens Lurie, art director Sara Reynolds and
senior designer Irene Vandervoort; Peter Buÿs and Anton Kras,
Jewish Historical Museum Library, Amsterdam;
René Kok, Netherlands Institute for War Documentation (NIOD),
Amsterdam; Gail G. Green, Miriam C. Drummonde;
Ann Zaiman; The Art Group; Frannie Friedman;
Joanne C. Fruchtman; Maida Barron; Mark Langrehr;
Lilian M.C. Randall; Ellen von Seggern Richter; Dottie Weintraub.
And with my loving thanks, Jeannie, Peter, Susan, Alan,
and especially Patrick.

———

Who was the woman
who wore the hat
I saw in the Jewish Museum?
What was she like?

Did she lie awake in the morning
and watch,
the way I did today,
as dawn brushed light through the sky?

Did she put cream in her coffee?

Did she put raisins
in her apple cake?

When the woman put on her hat,
did she tip the brim
just slightly?
        Did she like the way she looked
        with her hat down over one eye?

When did she buy it?
    I wonder.
And where did she wear it?
    Downtown, shopping with her
    daughter?
    Laughing with her little girl
    as they hurried along to Grandma's house?
    Happily walking home
    with her husband
    in the chill of evening?

I wonder
if she wore it
the day she left home the last time,
that cold, cold day in Amsterdam—
    that cold, cruel day in Amsterdam
    when the Jews were herded together
    and arrested in the Square.

There were islands of snow
on the rooftops—
there in the Square in the Jewish Quarter,
there by the darkened synagogue.

They all wore scarves and sweaters
and coats with collars turned up high.
And some wore hats
        as they knelt
        in the cold
        with their hands up over their heads.

How could she know
what to pack in her suitcase?
Or how many sweaters
to put on each of her children...

Was she pulled from her family
and lined up to be photographed—
        from the side,
        from the front,
        and then with her hat on her head?

Or did they even bother
with photographs
in Amsterdam—

      in their fierce, efficient rush
      to get the Jews on the trains—

It might have been my mother's hat.

It could have been my hat.

Or yours.

Who was the woman?

Whom did she love?

And did she put cream
in her coffee?

My questions are answered
by silence.

Yet I must ask them still.

For in my heart's searching
she lives on—
whoever she was,
whoever she was.

Author's Note

In the Jewish Historical Museum in Amsterdam I saw a woman's hat in a glass case. That's all there was—no label, no explanation, just a woman's hat on a stand. As I looked at it, I realized that this remnant, this quite ordinary hat, was all that remained of a woman's life.

I drew the hat in my sketchbook. Back home in my studio, I made a larger drawing, a self-portrait in which I was wearing the hat. Except for the winds of chance, I might have been that woman.

One day I wrote a short poem, wondering what she was like. I wrote other poems, with deepening awareness of my connection with this woman, and I realized these could become the text of a book.

I wanted the illustrations to look like fragments, conveying the sense of loss in the text. I crumpled my drawing papers, stained them with watercolor, and tore the edges. Copies of old photographs, taped onto my early sketches, added a sense of the period, and I decided to integrate them into my pencil drawings. For a year or so I drew portraits of Europeans from the 1930s and '40s, and I came to feel I knew them well. Some of them reminded me of people I've loved.

Before starting the final drawings, I went back to Amsterdam to sketch in the Square of the old Jewish Quarter and to do more research at the Museum. I had wanted to see the hat again, but it was gone.

In the making of this book, I've been enriched by reflections about a woman I will never know. I feel privileged to have been able to cherish her memory.

NANCY PATZ

Chronology of the Holocaust

January 30, 1933 — Adolf Hitler is appointed Chancellor of Germany.

April 1933 — Nationwide boycott of Jewish-owned businesses in Germany is carried out under Nazi leadership. Law excludes "non-Aryans" from government employment; Jewish civil servants, including university professors and school-teachers, are fired.

October 1934–November 1935 — Waves of arrests of homosexuals occur throughout Germany, continuing into November. Jehovah's Witnesses are banned from all civil service jobs and later arrested. Citizenship and racial laws are announced at the Nazi party rally in Nuremberg.

March 13, 1938 — Austria is annexed by Germany.

Winter 1938 — Nazis burn synagogues and loot Jewish homes and businesses in a nationwide pogrom called "Kristallnacht" ("Night of Broken Glass"). Nearly 30,000 German and Austrian men and women are jailed. All Jewish children are expelled from public schools. Segregated Jewish schools are created.

September 1, 1939 — Germany invades Poland; World War II begins.

February 22–23, 1941 — First arrest of Amsterdam Jews. "Hostages" are sent to "work camps," then Buchenwald, then Mauthausen.

1942 — Nazi extermination camps in occupied Poland at Auschwitz-Birkenau, Treblinka, Sobibór, Belżec, and Majdanek-Lublin begin mass murder of Jews in gas chambers.

June 1942 — Jews in France and Holland are required to wear identifying stars.

April 19–May 16, 1943 — Jews in the Warsaw ghetto resist with arms the Germans' attempt to deport them to the Nazi extermination camps.

March–July, 1944 — Germany occupies Hungary. Over 430,000 Hungarian Jews are deported to Auschwitz-Birkenau, where most of them are gassed.

January 1945 — Nazis evacuate Auschwitz and begin prisoners' "death marches" toward Germany. Soviet troops enter Auschwitz.

April–May 1945 — U.S. troops liberate survivors at Buchenwald, Dachau, and Mauthausen concentration camps.

May 7, 1945 — Germany surrenders, and the war ends in Europe.